BETTER LEFT UNSAID

"In the attitude of silence the soul finds the path in a clearer light, and what is elusive and deceptive resolves itself into crystal clearness. Our life is a long and arduous quest after Truth." ~Mahatma Gandhi

BETTER LEFT UNSAID

MICHAEL J. HOOVER

HANOVER POET LAUREATE, 2007-2009

XLIBRIS CORPORATION

To order additional copies of this book, contact:
Xlibris Corporation
1-888-795-4274
www.Xlibris.com
Orders@Xlibris.com
84860

To my lunatic affair with the moon, my muse,
who knows the smallest part of me.

CONTENTS

PARENTHETICAL MOMENTS

DISTANCE, DISSONANCE, DISCONNECT

ACKNOWLEDGMENTS

The poet most gratefully acknowledges Jamie, Bryan, and April, his children, who support his pursuit of the arts. He celebrates the inspiration, critique, and editorial expertise of Dana Larkin Sauers and the Hanover Poets, friend and poet Preston Mark Stone, and the editors of *Digges' Choice*, *Fledgling Rag*, *These Are the Times*, *One Tree, Many Branches 2001*, and *The Evening Sun* where many of these poems were first published, some in different form.

The Hanover Poet Laureate is thankful for the support of former Mayor of Hanover, Maggie Hormel, who proclaimed the post for the Greater Hanover Area in order to promote literacy. As such, Hanover became the first borough in Pennsylvania to so dedicate the position.

Cover photo by the poet who has learned that the two arts are inseparable twins in his Gemini life. Drawings by friend and artist Adrian Thomas Sauers.

FORWARD

Only someone with the adroit ability to confront life's complexities and fashion language's finer nuances as Michael Hoover, could have written the poetic compilation *Better Left Unsaid*.

The conscientiously arranged four divisions of *Echoing Absence, Ache of Appetite, Parenthetical Moments,* and *Distance, Dissonance and Disconnect* serve to create a progressive wave of meaning. These allow the reader to gently ride an accessible wake of understanding while, at times, suddenly being drug under into the realm of emotional leviathan.

Better Left Unsaid is an astute idiom that expands downward and outward in its meaning; the expression itself can connote many things simultaneously. Immediately, reasons and questions descend as to why one might not approach expression of a given idea or action, but just as quickly, the reader is reminded of the necessity to wade into the broad spaces where the clamor of silence and language collide. Here is a poetic statement of true, unabashed courage that dares plumb the waters of self and other-examination while also relating universal relevancy, a place where even "tainted certainty" must be acknowledged. **Better Left Unsaid** captivates the imagination and tears at the heart with its paradoxically articulated and volumed "vacancy," "hesitant intervals," and "delay at enjambment." Hoover's vision acknowledges an acceptance of "God's purse where there is no change," the statement existing as both resolve and challenge.

Hoover is a master of symbol, irony and tempered, periodically restrained tone; his commentary ranges from the serenade of heart's song through the satirical to the sardonic. A sensitive voice, sometimes tender, as well—at times, brazen, his words capture spaces few dare to describe. In this, his dualistic, Gemini nature emerges. Both created and creator, both recipient and provider, both prideful and humbled, Hoover escorts the reader on an odyssey of deep questioning and conflicts, no doubt drawn from his early Jesuit training, extensive reading and research.

It is not surprising that these poems command such a visual sense; Hoover evidently can reside in the moment. His images are at once clear and precise, largely formulated from his routine observational skills of lingering long on objects and ideas as well as his applied photographic experience. The works do not rest on the visual aspects alone but combine, also, both subtle and raking sounds to produce a genuinely holistic experience.

There is little to be unsaid about **Better Left Unsaid.**

Dana Larkin Sauers
7/28/2010

Better Left Unsaid

Listen to this poem's vacancy:
spaces echoing absence,
silhouettes of unstressed syllables,
the ghost-limb ache of appetite.

Hear each murmured metaphor,
breathed in hesitant intervals,
gorged on implication, asserting
promises whispered in ellipses . . .

How expectant lyrics fade—
each trace of allusion
and delay at enjambment
collude to say you are gone.

The tug of war between lines
creates parenthetical moments
and hearts apostrophized in
distance, dissonance, disconnect.

ECHOING ABSENCE

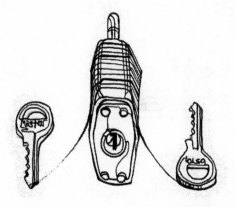

Less Than a Farthing

Sparrow on the sill,
stillness between us,
clear chasm of pane.

Snow shifts,
scrim of light against
a small kiss of dust
on the sash—

white print left
by the lips of God.

Common Ground

So many lives done—
undone like so many buttons of bone,
huge granite markers poking
through loopholes in cemetery lawn.

Unraveled families
rave at the ground,
turn to stone-cutters
to rival the permanent sky.

Names become more
than stories.
Faces, less
than words.
Sins, rain.

So much testament to toil.
So much soil from joy
pushing against prayers
in one great breath,
loosening the dirt.

Room Without a View

You insist that I lead
the soft-shoe shuffle of leaving
home, having spent time
in an arcade of second chances,
where hope was sleight of hand.

Rain fractures our view,
painting panes in perspiration.

Your cleared throat squeezes
my gut flaccid, like the dangling
last punch of a dance card.

KEENING MOON

Your waning weighs
each day as you ascend
burdened with summer.

Frozen eyes plead with an empty sky.
Your voiceless cry almost unseen;
orange blush pales to pastel yellow—

O sculpted lunacy,
marbled face
in seasonal sorrow,
don't fade to white this August night—
wait on the promise of harvest.

KEEPING ABREAST

Cells multiply where everything
is taken away; divide when
nothing adds up to something.

Living becomes the geometry
of holding on, the chemistry of change;
dying, the physics of letting go.

At the axis of bone and marrow,
where blood begins and can stop,
do only fractions of women remain?

CHIPPED PLATE

My sister pastels an ode to dreams
in pale clouds of creamy color,
baby-quilt streaks stitched in lines
along her life's unrhymed horizon.

In sister's chest hope rests,
a chipped plate, small keepsake,
fire begun at her love's genesis
for children and men, still aglow.

Her heart grows gibbous,
shock embossed across its face,
eyes wide sockets, dark pockets
of memory and motherhood.

Six More Weeks of Winter

Your lips unravel goodbye.
The unpredicted blizzard
clicks against the kitchen window.
Wind curses through curtains,
grim promise of a frigid night.

You demand that I be grounded—
be earth, when I am air;
water, where I am fire—

Our stew of better and worse
erupts into the fatal posture
of your face, the abrupt
furnace and ice in your eyes.

FOOD FOR THOUGHT

Robins quit their
quiet perch
with cheerful chirps
and scarlet appetites.

Early worms dance
among the blades of grass
proffer themselves
to be plucked and torn
for the peeps
ceaselessly cheeping
the timeless melody:

life is cheap
life is cheap
cheep
cheep.

GOLDEN GATE ESCAPE

Clouds lit in sunset
crisscross the city

mocking your looking back
going away, disappearing

in fog above the bay
as I gaze at crosscurrents below.

Crosshatched whitecaps flee
Alcatraz in madcap attempts

like your swim across the expanse,
risking all in turgid odyssey,

seeking shore like some forlorn
sea lion, lost and barking.

The Art of Self Pity

Sadness dawns, opaque haze
stretched and rubbed into sky

above a smudge of barren woods.
Whiskers of grass gone to seed

peek through fields of snow, a mottle
of soft stubble and pale shadows.

Orange bruise of sun intrudes
between the clouds and tree line

while one pathetic pine looks on,
a shrouded silhouette of protest

against another bitter day alone.

THIRTY-SIX THOUSAND FEET AFTER MOM'S DEATH

Night descends slowly, like understanding,
the great leveling out below—

Land dresses in shadows
and light belongs to those in flight.

Earth dims to darkness
like a faceless conversation;

Frozen explosions ascend,
ghosts of prayers and dreams.

Here, I embrace the expanse of you
as a rainbow flattens into gold.

God remains an insomniac craving rest,
if only creation could pause without ending.

ACHE OF APPETITE

HALF LIVES

A fine line divides the half-moons
of what we know and hope.

Safest and most vulnerable:
Hamlet's curse, Eden's hanging fruit.

Level crescent at liquid and air;
balance of a white lie and a half-kiss.

Hesitation is the temperature fire begins to freeze.
Are we waning or waxing, midnight or noon?

There's no time to what if, maybe, or think twice.
Will you take my hand or must I take half your life?

A KILLER POEM

I want to be a poem hung in a pouch
awaiting David's hand to heft me,

be swung in a sling, given wings,
flung to some Philistine's face,

cracking cranium, breaking brow,
creating chasm wide enough

to ponder the power of pebble
launched in prayer, mumbled verse,

ancient mantra turning toy to weapon,
sacred chant transforming boy to man:

stone
      palm
            string
                  psalm
                        sting
                              bone.

FALLING

Gliding on a swing, we lock eyes
in tilted wonder, a seasonal question
rising out of crisp leaves in the yard:
will coming days be calm or wintry wild?

We ponder summer's found and lost moments:
licorice raindrops, black pearls of joy's mist.

Turning from the lingering sun,
we unhinge ourselves while the swing,
swaying still, invites us to ride
an autumn afternoon again.

FADING BLUSH

Outside, flowers sigh in dying hues,
lure bees and butterflies
with memory of nectar and honey.

Within, peonies perch above
a poem to the sky in your eyes,
reflection of the heaven in you.

You smile, then comment,
your voice an octave higher,
dimples not quite so deep,
face holding a mere hint of heat.

You make the customary
after-coffee-gotta-go chirp,
shape I love you with parting lips,
wave and waltz away, swaying hips.

Fading flowers dance upon your dress
as light plays red with your brunette,
while I am left on my steps, in sunset.

ON ANY SUNDAY

Three pews removed,
I watch morning strike

your bare arms and hair
through the stained glass

of triumphant Gabriel,
whose horn gleams golden

and posture remains erect.
Yellow glides along the curve

of your shoulder, ends where skin
meets the silk of your dress.

A halo glows about your head
like the magnet of a fragrance

imagined in briefly nestling there.
You caress the down on your neck,

fingers spread a chill among shadows.
You sense something from behind,

something subtle, like light, like breath.

Waiting for Turkey

The day thaws slowly.
Gray skies break into the blue
in your eyes peeking over the horizon
of your glass while their twin smiles
beget a blush in the dim light.

A fire gently rages against the snow.
Music breathes into the room.
The fragrance of a seasoned turkey
warms us in a spiritually sensual way.

Outside, trapped mountain air
travels beneath sheets of ice,
resembling dark sperm
in a wavy search for home,
following gravity's lead
into uncertain pools below.

BREAKFAST INSTEAD

You look for passion
and I make waffles—
thick, syrupy, warm as love.

You paint poppies
and a nude curled in the grass,
her arched back to the viewer.

And I serve seconds,
sweeter than a first kiss,
tasting morning still on my lips.

Love's Tongue

Babel of whispers, laughter:
snippets of conversation
echo along a sidewalk,
soften into wedding soup,
hot tea and meditation.

Eyes peer through steam,
lips sip at ceramic rims;
fingers stretch to touch
under a crescent moon
pulling the reluctant tide.

YELLOW AMBUSH

Two bright finches, a couple
in love with thistles and sun,
among butterflies and winnowing seeds,
fill themselves, harvest the moment,
while petals dance to the ground
in love-me-love-me-not swirls . . .

POOL OF MOON

Diana dives without hesitation
into her reflection; she

swims in my melancholy,
buoyed by her laughter,

and blushes in defiance of her glow.
Her faint silhouette dances above me.

God's brazen marionette
mocks my ensnared desire.

She transforms invocation
to the soft breath of a poem,

eulogy to the distance
between huntress and prey.

LAZARUS COMES OUT

> . . . *Jesus called out in a loud voice, "Lazarus, come out!"* . . .
> John 11:43

You arouse me
from tattered dreams of grief.

I rise, rapt, unraveling,
gravely aching for simplicity:
an untethered kiss,
a warm sip of morning,
some revelation of heaven.

You weave flaxen moonlight
from spun, divine lunacy;
I want to strip off this linen,
melt in a lover's silken touch,
loosen one heart with my song.

I am too lame to speak,
too blind to understand
your invitation to live or my urge
to dance instead with the dying.

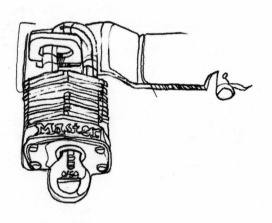

PARENTHETICAL MOMENTS

DANCING WITH ALISON

Your mother wit contends
with wishes for the kids
when you have gone away.

You squint against the blur
of all that might have been
and take my arm to climb
the slope behind the shed.

I move some clay and stone.
We pot the plants from friends
because, you say, someone
will see them bloom one day.

Our embrace is final, feral,
more support than letting go,
your frame a swaying lotus stem
bearing its enchanted blossom.

We stand, ungraceful dancers,
wait for God's distant do-si-do
so you can whirl into heaven,

as I turn from your little-girl
grin and invitation to follow.

MICHAEL J. HOOVER

COMMUNION

Across the piazza from Duomo
people fidget like pigeons,
fixed on destination—Pisa, Firenze,
someplace beyond binario duo,
somewhere other than home.

Blind man in a white shirt,
bolo tie, dress shoes, puffs
a cigar stub, waving a wand
to match his crisp cadence
and patent leather posture.

Women urge their mothers
arm-in-arm around the promenade,
purses swinging in late afternoon.
Children play among ancient shrubs.
Men on benches knit their narratives.

Shutters make shadow wings
on yellow and salmon stucco.
Beneath sheets and lingerie,
phrases linger above slate streets
pocked by pageantry, commerce, war.

MOSAIC

My life is cut stained glass,
a puzzle of color to ponder:
sharp shapes, curling curves—
stems and blossoms of possibility,
unscented flowers, driftless clouds,
a frozen sun in a breathless sky.
Yet you come to worship the art
the light begets, sensing completion
in the broken, leaden pieces.

HARRY'S AVIARY

Owls crowd your never-been-cleaned,
heavy-draped rooms: predatory lamps,
stark glares over edges of picture frames,
vigilant figurines, carved handle on the ceiling
fan's pull chain. Even a yellow-eyed bed throw.

Your days link in iceless whiskey,
smoke-rings from discount cigarettes.
Folk wisdom reveals a remedy
for drunkenness is raw owl eggs,
nailing up owl's wings wards off lightning.

You sleep while chicken fries
in an cast iron skillet and wake,
as flames rise from the char, fly,
talons open, in a flurry of curtains.

MY MUSE HAS NO STRINGS

High over fences, we take in distance.
Clouds form blue holes and fairy tale scenery.

Nose at my shoulder, you whisper
time is thread hemming eternity.

Our kite's tail, you spin us above
thickets of conflict and criticism.

Cross braced, we renounce
envious ground, soar free.

KISS

Tart
becomes
the lemon's
sweet desire—

the pull from which
attached lips
cannot
part.

SPIDER AND BUTTERFLY

Looming, he spins;
fluttering, she weaves.
He's science; she's art.

He plucks at strings,
frets his silent melody
with a venomous heart.

She sings of sky and sun,
sailing trails of whimsy
upon invented current.

Preying, he meditates;
straying, she sashays
toward the dark center
of a gossamer flower,
to the pearly snare
of his fatal embrace.

MICHAEL J. HOOVER

ABOUT FACE: TWO VIEWS

on Edward Hopper's *Sea Watchers*

I

Sunrise of discontent;
he, leaning on thighs;
she, all sanguine sighs,
content to remain intent.

Waves chant promises,
blush at dawn's curve,
offer morning like a trophy
below a new-born sky.

II

Sun sets on discontent;
him, all elbows and thighs,
her, sagging sighs,
intent to remain content.

Surf pounds a dirge
under flamingo clouds
stretched into forms
tainted by certainty.

CAFÉ FRAGMENT

You ride the rhythm of voices,
the strum of a heart's guitar.
Humdrum art stares from walls,
words dissolve into chatter.

The set waxes kaleidoscopic:
perfect fractal of what matters
in the web of lyrics and laughter.

Songs end in fretting fingers
dancing along taut strings.
Memories stir and linger,
souls spill freely onto tables.

Spoons clink, cartoon porcelain
fish scales on a thinly frozen lake.
Applause fades to an aching pause.

You swirl burnt umber dregs
at the bottom of your cup.

MICHAEL J. HOOVER

MAKING SENSE

I see faces
in stone and rock
in proud thorns and thick bark
in the swell over boulders of a creek grown to river.

I smell gravity
below moss and churned earth
under thickets and decay
beneath eroding banks where ground and water marry.

I hear the language
of insects, birds, and rodents
weak current along a warm connection
giving voice to roiling pulse.

I taste light
beyond stars and caverns
in stories behind ancient eyes
beside city curbs teeming with grit and broken lives.

I touch joy
in freshly dug dirt
among songs whispered in cornfields
inside God's purse where there is no change.

STARVED FOR ATTENTION

A child's final sigh rises skyward;
another psalm with no reply.

In upturned hands in outstretched prayer,
innocence again is proffered to a famished will.

And God is breathing all creation in obesely,
taking back the gift to every mother given.

Her tacit shriek, silent hallowed shout,
a grimly veiled and barefaced appeal:

Don't let this humble sacrifice be pleasing, and
to his cradle grave she bears her blameless babe,

All she has to give for all she has been given,
a never ending end where everything's forgiven.

WESTERN PRESENT

Jellied flesh circle pockets
scooped from massive rock.
The Pacific recedes into fog,
exposes pools of ocean jewels:
sea stars frozen in mid-gesture,
lissome anemone beckoning,
ancient boulders encrusted
in barnacle songs of stone.

Below the ridge meadows open,
glaciers carve a crooked horizon,
pines stretch in one green chorus,
streams vie with wind for attention.
The smell of sun is blue off faces
of mountains. The ubiquitous silence
of God descends upon alpine valleys.

BLOOD FROM WINE

Gethsemane provides a trace of peace
as you soliloquize in a thirst to persevere.

Friends leave you at the teeth of faith,
to contemplate the weight of miracle.

Praying over possibility,
you're left to self-reliance.

Comrades cluster under trees, rocks
around a crucifix or underneath a temple.

Shadows laugh, concelebrate despair
and destiny with silver and a kiss.

You see from dust you must leave,
poets unseal the word left for dead,

reveal the wine embalmed behind a stone
and fill each vessel with poems of blood.

DISTANCE, DISSONANCE, DISCONNECT

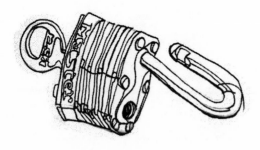

POETRY IS NO PICNIC

Algae undulates beneath
decayed trees, too rooted
in what is shore.

Clouds swarm
like crowded thoughts;
people, like windblown debris.

An empty plastic cup
beckons one yellow jacket
to what instinct says
is more than sufficient.

In gluttonous buzz
the insect, like a poet,
curbs an urge to alert the nest,
indulges, instead, in solitary sin.

Hell's Beltway,

Where Exits Pass Like Rosary Beads

*Sniper attacks took place during three weeks in October 2002
in Washington, D.C., Maryland, and Virginia. Ten people were
killed and three others critically injured.*

Any burning bush would be nice.

Some divination for the hundreds
of thousands of panicked prayers
said at pumps and in parking lots.

Some message from beyond the interstate.

Instead, a bead is drawn on unwary quarry
as God, an absentee landlord, demands the rent.

A single degree of separation begins
its concentricity, its business of circumvention,
targeting markets, sniping customers.

Crosshairs creep into focus, bullets spiral down the barrel
like leaden dancers pirouetting in a ballet of steel and flesh.

A fragmented neuropath, whose brain
is a braided crown of pain and cruelty,
a visceral visionary, whose scarf
is wound too tight about the head,
marks his marks, a disassembled mosaic
of bones and tarot cards tossed madly in the air.

SISYPHUS RECYCLED

You come crookedly
down the street again
writhing along, pushing
the cart before you
as an ant does a morsel,

like in a Beckett play
where pointedly pointless
conversations
search for the ends
of ropes.

And when,
in orange suspenders,
you stop at each
can to root,
ever seeking treasure
in the depth of discards,

your stubble betrays
your home in the park
where benches are as scarce
as happy endings.

Say It Again, Uncle Sam

I am not ditto I am not ditto I am
not ditto but I am da funk, da funk.

I am not ditto nor ditto nor
any defunct ditto machine
gun, firing silence
into minds, cavernous mines
dittoing echoes, echoing dittos.

I'm friendly, barbaric, and kind—
a bibulous Biblicist, homophobic homilist—
bibliophobic and blind,
misanthropic, Messianic,
et cetera, ditto, et cetera.

Hey, ditto, ditto dum, ditto dee.
I pledge allegiance to the Almighty
dollar; in our flag we trust, united,
untied, nuclear and unclear—just like Sam
to a dyslexic Hispanic simply means
more, ditto more and ditto more.

MY EX-JAMES DEAN COMPLEX

What got into me to follow the bad boys—
to live my secret life—
create and hide my sins, unconfessed;
challenge shame for the thrill of being chased,
the power of knowing what few others knew,
the sake of doing what was unexpected?

Is this the fantasy of every boy
or of those led astray, shown the way
down the path of daring and danger?

I relish risks of children and artists,
love the turns in my own writing:
its power to provoke indulgence,
tempt experiment and exposure,
even expulsion from the paradise
of expectation and contentment.

MICHAEL J. HOOVER

PETTING ZOO

Caught creating chaos,
a pedagogue shakes
his empty fist at Piety,
decrying to every child
mea maxima culpa and
can we make up again?

Cries rise like feathers after a kill,
amid hawkish cawing, clawing air,
an angel's prayer not to be prey.

Each crouches, fetal in his own shadow,
awaiting the talons of some petty god.

STONES AND FEATHERS

At rock bottom
current smoothes
edges cracked by
landslides and torrents
of black sky.

At the end of a rope,
bristly, knotted strands
cling to never-let-go,
twisted in tradition,
entwined in tomorrow.

When wells run dry,
mud cakes, then flakes;
feathery chips wait
for wind to make
the dust of creation.

A phoenix rises out of
cremated angels—
millstones encircle
necks of neglect, flung into
the avalanche of abundance.

Wings

Show me the dark reward of lying.
To say to a tag-a-long brother,
Mom is calling. You had better go.
Help me escape his thick sobs,
sick at his hero's cowardice.

Trespass with me across boggy
fields to toss two-handed rocks
into soggy red clay. Smooth
my stomach's churning stones.

Teach me the chills in pinching
beetles' wings, to watch them
drop to a creek trying to fly
from the ledge of a bridge,
before my instinct takes hold.

SPRING CLEANING

Life broken into drawers.
Micro-biographies of discards, get-to's, and save-these:
a smattering of tattered snapshots, neglected notes,
a small vault of keys without locks, tack-pins for lost causes,
a keep of obsolete receipts, a cache of collectible coins;
invalid phone numbers, broken-pointed pencils,
one dead AA, a hoarded pen hardened in the artery,
an assembly of unused parts, assorted cards from the kids—
forgotten remembrances: a tomb for trash and heirlooms;
sepulcher of treasure doomed to scrap or resurrection.

On the Line

She hangs yellow-gray undershirts,
moth wings flapping in the sun,
matching the mucus ever
clumped just above his lips.
He jabbers about brown juniper,
jabbing his cane at the decay.

Empty clothesline dips twice,
a contour of drooping breasts,
bared for neighbors to see,
huge u's with clothespin nipples,
mocking motherhood, sagging
under dreams wrung dry.

Meals from pared cash and
vegetables, thrown into salads—
unhungry husband becomes
a wilted carrot, whiskers wild
root hairs he cannot see to shave.

She unhangs the only outerwear
he will hang upon himself
these endless days of dying

while she murmurs about the past
when love was uncomplicated,
children danced among fallen apples,
and clean clothes easily pleased a man.

The breeze shifts, the landscape responds.
Everything dead appears alive under the air's caress.
Sheets undulate on the line with more life
than the man flailing in their floral waves
on his way to the garden where
hope, God's compost, lies.

MICHAEL J. HOOVER

COMING APART AT WHAT SEEMS

A torch wavers in night breeze
while frogs croon and June bugs
dance above the moon's light
reflected in what used to be.

A woman broods in silhouette
bare elbows on bare knees—
hands, cool cups collecting
the past pouring from her eyes.

Crickets mesmerize fireflies
wrestling the fresh dew—
a green scent rises in
harmony with darkness.

The woman glances upward,
universe a shade of gloom,
her heart, a pendulum, swaying
in the cage of what will be.

Two birds coo good-night
into the rustle of deepening dusk
as stars chant their ancient chorus
and clouds slip a veil across the sky.

In Praise of Laceration

Clean operation, they say,
the poem keenly cut
from my head to tow
the lines yet unwritten,
good as dead.

Small incision,
malignant language
neatly bagged,
extracted to exact
an empirical toll.

Biopsy says words
will metathesize,
spread into prose,
perhaps a poison pen letter.

MICHAEL J. HOOVER

THE ISCARIOT CODE IN HAIKU

Judas, the poet,
earns silver for golden words
whispered as a kiss.

He pens a red ode
etched among the stones and sand
his back to the sun:

Kissed my friend, Jesus,
thirty pieces of silver—
suicide haiku.

Judas sings solo
each of thirty lines he wrote—
pharisitic rag.

Despair seeks a tree
betrayal by cross and nails—
crucifixion blues.

Exchanges his friend
for a pocketful of fame
and a lone tree limb.

Still swings in sunlight
bloated, hollow piñata—
broken by God's stick.

Edwards Brothers,Inc!
Thorofare, NJ 08086
06 December, 2010
BA2010340